Behemoth

Also by Bruce Bond:

Scar

The Calling

Words Written Against the Walls of the City

Plurality and the Poetics of Self

Frankenstein's Children

Rise and Fall of the Lesser Sun Gods

Dear Reader

Blackout Starlight: New and Selected Poems: 1997–2015

Sacrum

Gold Bee

*Immanent Distance: Poetry and the Metaphysics
of the Near at Hand*

Black Anthem

For the Lost Cathedral

The Other Sky

Choir of the Wells

The Visible

Peal

Blind Rain

Cinder

The Throats of Narcissus

Radiography

Behemoth

POEMS

Bruce Bond

WINNER OF THE NEW CRITERION POETRY PRIZE

Criterion Books
NEW YORK

BEHEMOTH. Copyright © 2021 by Bruce Bond. All rights reserved. No part of this publication may be reproduced, stored in a retrieval system, or transmitted, in any form or by any means, electronic, mechanical, photocopying, recording, or otherwise, without the prior written permission of Criterion Books, 900 Broadway, Suite 602, New York, NY 10003.

First American edition published in 2021 by Criterion Books, an imprint of Encounter Books, an activity of Encounter for Culture and Education, Inc., a nonprofit, tax-exempt corporation.
www.newcriterion.com/poetryprize

Library of Congress Cataloging-in-Publication Data

Names: Bond, Bruce, 1954– author.
Title: Behemoth / Bruce Bond.
Description: First American edition. | New York : Criterion Books, 2021. | Identifiers: LCCN 2020024880 | ISBN 9781641771443 (cloth)
Subjects: LCGFT: Poetry.
Classification: LCC PS3552.O5943 B44 2021 | DDC 811/.54–dc23
LC record available at https://lccn.loc.gov/2020024880

Contents

I

Border	3
Parkland	9
Proof	10
Bronze	11
Wall	13
Skull	14
Oracle	16

II

Swan	21
Mallarmé	27
Poe	28
Zion	30
Stone	31
The Words	32
Vanitas	34

III

Angel	*37*
Calvary	*39*
Air	*41*
Fire Scripture	*44*
Sun	*46*
Behemoth	*48*

Acknowledgments

The author would like to thank the editors of the following journals in which these poems previously appeared: *Agni*, *The Common*, *Gettysburg Review*, *The Hopkins Review*, *Image*, *Iron Horse Review*, *Literary Matters*, *Narrative*, *Plume*, *and St. Katherine Review*. Also, many thanks to the Association of Literary Scholars, Critics, and Writers for selecting the poem "Skull" as winner of the Meringoff Prize.

Behemoth

A soldier learns
To bear the silver weight
Where in his head the fire is most alive.

—Anthony Hecht, "The Plate"

I

Border

1.

Begin with a face, this casting pool set in bone,
      where the other faces graze the surface
and slide, and who remembers what it was to begin,
      who back then, if anyone, we were.
Always the shroud of a stranger across the chill
      of the looking glass, and I am looking more
and more like my father and know I never get there.
      The face on television says, we should open gates
to us and ours alone, and somewhere a lonely man
      says, yes, I feel that way. And one flame
flows into another, and who can tell them apart.
      Who has not filled the empty holy landscape
of the margins. Everywhere the smoke of cities
      and exclusionary spaces, where if you knock
the bodies on video feeds they sound like glass.
      What a sound bite needs is a larger story with small
and smaller pieces, a girl, say, who stares
      into the camera before the pan and fade,
though we know she is out there, the face among faces,
      the Eucharist of imagined life.

2.

Let me begin again. Time is priceless,
        and we are always in the middle
of some covert conflict somewhere, caught
        in the river of thousands pouring into thousands,
gathering in the makeshift city of widows
        and tents, and there are limits to a body,
a nation, a sea. There are rivers drawn as mirages are
        across the names of other waters,
and what is the use of words and images that come
        so far and no farther, of the protest
song and broken camera abandoned in the sand.
        Whose grains are these in the storm
blown back across our footsteps,
        where the new planes carry their payload,
undetected, and have no people in them.
        The words *Christian* or *fire* or *covert conflict*
have no people either, only jaws
        to consume the bread of imagined life.
And as we talk, the body of us, in us, divides—
        it must—longing to be whole.

3.

Long ago they cut my father's body open to accept
    the harvest of a stranger's heart.
When he woke, the hospital room smelled of chrome
    and disinfectant, and he thought,
surely this is paradise, and his palpitations
    spiked. Somewhere there is a flashlight
in the tunnel of your chest, a voice that cries,
    who's there, and no one answers. In time,
it says less and less, camouflaged in fibers;
    the beam dims; words go deaf; the gape
of the ribcage swallows the Eucharist
    in silence. Who is left to say where the stranger
draws its boundaries. Vein after vein
    nets the vital muscle, and even the blood
of the incision is, as they say, connective tissue.
    The bruise shade of the liver,
the spleen, the thyroid that is an outpost of the brain,
    they are all braided like strangers
at the foot of a tower on fire. Like anger
    flowing into anger and who can tell them apart.

4.

America has no face. Let me begin again.
    It is neither driver nor the mother
on the bus who pulls the string, not the chime,
    not the echo, never the house
particular with debt and pills and bad news
    from Ferguson or Beirut or some such holy land,
and the candidate who would wear our features says,
    I open my heart, but homes are homes,
and I turn on him and lock my door behind me.
    A Christian nation has no Christ,
and Christ no nation. I am looking
    for a better song. I cast my vote
into the water to watch it slice across the larger picture.
    One nation under God, a child says.
Beneath her hand, the anonymity of the personal,
    the vital muscle, the fist, the first
to fear, the last to explain. Lord of the body,
    peerless, eyeless, compelled.
I search the names on the ballot for the nameless.
    I make my pledge.

5.

To judge another's words by what we know about the speaker
    is to know neither speaker nor word.
So says a schoolbook a boy finds boring
    and then he gets a beating from two strangers,
and as he hangs by his hair in the grasp of one,
    he says nothing, he is losing faith in words,
he goes home and, once again, nothing, and over dinner,
    nothing, and night after night, he lies
awake, and nothing comes. I am looking for a better song,
    the kind that moves across the borders
in the old language. Or wades against the water
    beneath the guns of the lookout, and what remains is
the vast unfathomed reaches of a sky. I am sorry
    for everything I did and did not do,
I told my father in the end, and he was confused.
    I still see that face among the many he wore,
buried in a music I could not hear, and I needed
    my own to hear it. It felt enormous, this tune, and I
was small and smaller, and he was crossing over,
    and he looked at me, my grief, as if it were a stranger.

6.

In the song of the Eucharist of imagined life,
        a girl stares into the camera, and the liquidation
of eyes and money spills from the anonymity
        of the personal into the great collection plate.
Protesters take their guitars to the river, and one
        tune flows into another, and whatever music does
and does not do, the girl who sings feels small and smaller,
        and who are we to know. Somewhere
a theorist is writing a paper and feels it too: the longing
        for greater detail, larger scope. Somewhere
a man eats the bread and feels absolved and little
        changes or all things small and who are we to know.
Begin with a face. Yours or another's. Little changes
        gather downstream, beneath the eyes, and they have seen it,
the power of a song, how it just might pull a body through
        the mirror, out some painful story or door,
into another. The refugees' song carries something
        of language over the river, and the river closes behind them
like a wound. It forgets. And in the song you hear it
        running. And sometimes in their eyes, you see.

Parkland

After the killing, evangelist Jim Bakker
saw God in camouflage with a hunting vest
and semi-automatic rifle, and he read
the dream the way some do a murderous
flood or autocrat or anomaly of crows,
as a manifest of blood and righteousness
to fill each eye with its accursed share.
Our Lord wants his teachers to bear arms,
he said to whatever flock remained, now
that prison was behind him, the reckoning
ahead. No doubt he knew a thing or two
of hell, angry in his sleep, not knowing why,
suffering still the disavowal of his peers,
and his poor heart, muscular and blue
with self-abuse, skimmed a little bitterness
off and hid the profits, off-book, offshore.
What is any dream if not the brain calling
to another self, unsure who, what exile
of Jerusalem longing to join the others.
The shooter was a loner—they always are—
but to the bullied and confused, he just
might be the one who understands, as well
as any child, what it is to feel unseen,
unheeded, camouflaged in fire and angels.

Proof

Monasteries who claimed sole possession
of a savior's foreskin must have known,
a holy thing is money, and so, they came,
pilgrims from the wetlands of the plague.
They knelt, gave alms, received what solace
the feeble in flesh and spirit can expect.
Perhaps a couple thought of it as funny.
And why not. Every idol is a toy.
It always was. When I was a child,
I talked to them, for them. I do it still.
Photographs arranged on shelves just so,
they know. Life is lonely out there
without a past save the one you give
to things that speak the language of your giving.
And so you listen, talk, hear a clearer
rationale for lying to your mother
at the end, pretending that you know
the blood of the covenant is lovely
and alive, in all that she becomes.
However heartsick the fetish or allegiance,
the foreskin was someone's after all.
I want to say a mother wept for joy.
If she opened a window on a meadow
that bled a brighter April than those on earth,
still, when I think of her, I think of earth.
I see her child's cry in the poppies,
the mohel's scalpel at the break of dawn.
Why pray for the dead if not for this,
for God's speed on their journey home
beneath the burden of the proof they bear.

Bronze

      Tower bells beat the door
of the sky and so call those who hear
the toll of marriage or mourning or time
passing, before the bronze goes still.
Today I hear all those calls at once,
leaning from the chamber—a rapture
that bears, I know, a given message,
though I like to think the music has its own.
So too its own cloud swept through
the parapet, where the temple scaffolds
rise and fall over the face and stones
of a great design, the one I never see.
I, a mongrel, married a Jew, my table
crowned in candles whose light and honey
smokes the air, and they are not mine,
these dispensations echoed at the altar,
not mine, the music of my home,
though it marries me to the silence after.
Call me a follower then, a mute observer,
a bit of stone against the larger burden.
I married a battered child, the girl
in her broken by a stranger again
and again like a wave inside a shell.
Whenever I hear bells, I think of this,
unable to say what needs to be said
or hear the broken silence when it speaks.
Nights I am awakened by her breathing,
and still I dream. Still her heart beats
its bronze against a sky I cannot enter.

And when she moans, I shake her gently.
It's okay, I answer. That's all it takes.
A stage whisper, and she mumbles, *thank you, love you,* without opening her eyes.

Wall

Too broadly drawn for any one perspective,
it will wear our silhouettes the way
a contract wears its ink, a bomb-site
its safety glass, a widow the veil that weds her
once again. It will serve as one more
instrument of faith, come to outsource
our debts to another nation, our wounds
to eyes for whom everything is wounded.
A new sun is speeding our direction,
so can you blame us, if we cannot look
or look away, if we tell ourselves we will
get this right, raise a barricade of swords
into its resting place, crowned in wire,
where a border guard walks on our behalf,
when we are somewhere, safe, far as day
from the circle of suffering that offers
refuge to our monsters. And if we strike
a door or clause or beer on the counter
or the father who struck us first, once,
can we agree. Can we say the edifice,
however disinterested, disgraced, painted
over in mists of disenfranchised anger,
will be beautiful and strong, tall enough
to break a neck, if, God forbid, it must.
It will call our little lambs from their home
theaters of good behavior, to give them
a harder template for their fears, a place
to bear the cocks and crosses of two worlds now,
and its shadow will list from side to side.

Skull

The thrill ride with a skull at the crest
of the mountain is pouring a waterfall
through each eye, a gush too ludicrous
for tears, however desperate to be seen,
to join the sad extravagance of things
that fall. A part of me is always falling.
Ever pouring into the world, as light
that pours into pools. And who can
tear the water from the eye, the sky
from the water, the cry from the boy.
A child in the roller coaster rounds
its precipice, and his heart pounds stop
or go or what the hell. Impossible
to say if fear houses some illusion,
or the illusion a fear, or ecstasy sets
the house on fire, as the railcar plunges
through the spray, and the dream is over.
If I pretend too easily or not enough,
I know I have lost my balance, falling
as one who has a falling out with life
itself, who sleeps too much or not at all.
The water in the eye of the skull mists
the kids in line below, and the screams
of joy obscure the real cry in the crowd.
I saw a Cyclops once that ate a head,
and my father took me from the dark
of the theater to the sunlit lobby
and said, it's not real, it's only a movie,
and I wondered if he knew what I knew.

I was so tender and small, I could fit
through the hole in last night's dream, so
slow to close, and silent as a fontanel.
All my life the brain lay hidden away.
No wonder it's a stranger, says the brain.
A child leaves home to conceive a home,
a shelter in the horror and the wild,
and know so little about it, as if unknowing
were the alpha and omega of home,
the shadow that seals the marriage kiss,
a farewell so constant it has the stillness
of those in shock, when the car hood steams
and the one you were has yet to arrive.
Skulls are nothing to me. I admit.
I rarely see them in my friends, and if
I do, I am not listening. But a wound,
a wound is a mirror, and you know it
when you see it, when it tremors the part
that cannot explain, or punishes a toy
in silence, or opens a womb to let
the stranger out. What the mirror takes,
it gives back a little older, an exile
of how you knew yourself and the others
and the glass that is so much water over
the mountain, only now prepared to hear
a father, it's not real, and marvel at how
deep he slept without a dream come dawn.
Only now, you close your eyes, as he
closed his taking with him the real cry
in the rapture. And in the blood that is
yours alone, the suffering that never is.

Oracle

A broken rib could be the sign
that stabs a little when you breathe,
long after the boy who beat you
goes free, and still you keep him
near, in the breathing chamber,
the way a jilted lover keeps watch.
Every time you touch the bruise,
you hold a knife to your chest,
and as the bone mends, it closes
a coffin that might be tender,
years later. You bear the scar,
the way a mountain road bears
a cross. It will become you,
advise you, inflect your name
with an ember of suspicion.
As you grow large, it will grow
larger. It will be everywhere.
Like the moan of the foghorn
in a meadow of waves before
the aching of the mist goes clear.
Nothing to see here, an officer
says, binding the crime in tape,
and still you stare. Still as a candle
whose fire is your blessing now,
you who feel and do not feel,
as children might a bit of shame
for something dreamt, forgotten,
or misplaced. Just today, you felt
a change on the horizon. A smell

of metal or blood or something
burning, something in the wind,
a whispered name, gone nameless,
dragged across the windshields
of the wrecking yard, barbed
in wire, where a guard-dog sleeps,
beneath the lock and chain, he sleeps,
and the weather calls for rain.

II

Swan

Here, in this writing chamber,
with its desk set, vase of ink,
the faint depressions of the blotter
lit with oil harvested at sea;
our weary insomniac, John
Keats, is not well, though he
cannot know this yet, what
we know, how the story ends.
He cannot see us, his future,
let in a draft from the highlands
and whisper of his ailment.
He is too busy looking out
on a world that is half-dark,
half-garden and a ghost-reflection
of the self who, mesmerized
by silence, marks the dying fall
of poems in an empty room,
to hear in words the emptiness.
It is a piece he will not finish,
though he works night into day
talking with disconsolate gods
bereft of acolytes and a sense
of humor. That said, his speaker,
our sole avatar, barely speaks,
though all the pantheon is there
on the vine-beleaguered portico,
each a scrap of marble in a plot
whose civic matrix is dismantled,
whose mortar mists at daybreak,

where cobbles of the otherworld
jewel against the bright onset.
It will be life to see them, he writes,
but what he sees he sees through
like a window laid across a stand
of oak whose unheard tunes are
sweeter, clearer, he tells himself,
whose story comes to a stream made
of glaciers in decline, goliaths
of weather and the long clear pull
of its turbulence, downstream.
Once men walked across the water,
and children followed, and the willows
leaned down like lions to the lyre.
Women traced their silhouettes
on the walls of caves, and when
they died, the shadows remained
and drew our shadows, in kind, to them.
as if our death had met its match.
The bodies of the killing fields
would not be still and rose the way
tidal waters do and exalted tones
as their horrors rise, undaunted.
Iron from the veins of leopards
poured over the lips of cataracts,
and the names they bore were a river's
name, and their god a river still.

***

When I was a kid, I had a puppet,
a lion with one eye, his ear
eaten by rain or rot or some
corrosive creature. A castaway
I found in the bushes, or he
found me, his face half-alive,
the other half-blind, and I laid
my voice in the darker portion.
What was that you lost, my friend
leaned in to ask me, *that key
to the boathouse, life before life,
that lamentation in the ocean.*
He was talking about a dream
I had, the childhood I left,
my other father and the small
red pail of sand, and then. I woke.
A wave rolled through my chest.
It broke and, in the silence, roared.
Tonight, in the mausoleum
stillness, as day burns down its house
of glass and calls it *progress*,
my wife lights a Shabbat candle,
and I see the smoke her mother
saw, the ovens of the war years,
their ecstasies of filth and cinders.
*Beauty overpowers all other
considerations*, the writer writes,
and then he hears a gold bell
in a nearby room and answers
with bowls of mangoes and broth
and towels to wipe the discharge

from his brother's lip. His gods
grow more and more contagious,
the air metallic, the verses more
difficult to finish, though he swears
an oath. He breathes into the corpse
of earth to swell the core, to raise
a fountainhead of dolls and monsters.

***

Terror writes what terror burns,
each dawn, and the sun gods die,
and the sky moves still. Clouds tear
like hands from a helicopter rope.
So what is lost, or spent, what
superannuations of sunk realms.
What gems inside the marble
forehead of the heroine if not
the theater dark that holds her
to us. Ask the man who coughs
blood into his brother's name.
Blood dries, the name continues.
In a day or two, it pales, it dries,
all things drawn through the mirror
of each other. Remember me,
says the movie that cannot move
beyond its dull montage: stone
lion, stone lamb, stoned retirement
home and boy who is its gardener.

You could live this way for years,
in a graveyard of the stars, writing
melancholic odes with real wine
in them. A drowsy numbness could
pain your sense, until one night
in the labyrinths of Rome, you
lose your way. The café awnings
fold their wings in the cold facade,
and a downpour drowns your coat
and hair. When a god dies, what then.
You could submit to starvations
and bleedings, the terrible science
romance is made of, and find comfort
in the company. And why not.
Go on. Make them fabulous,
these Athenas dying of neglect,
their robes in ribbons, luxurious
as rope that floats above the factories.
Make them idols out of beach
glass and expenditures of breath
grown deep and weary from the journey.
Sometimes the more merciful view
is a porch in ruins. *The beauty
of decaying things.* On the far side
of the world, there is a word for that,
for rust that eats across the signage.
A word for the heads of flowers
bent beneath the burden of light,
for the brittle legs of bees,
green striations of a stream
gone dry, a word for the scratch

of hieroglyphic on the gold-plate
tomb that no one understands.
A word for the father when he
has no words, but looks out on
the sea with a voice that makes
no sense, and, yes, I nodded, yes.
The red door of the eye swings
wide to say, you too, come, sit.
I can't sleep either. Dead lions,
patriots, letters on the far side
of the suffering that makes them
sing, come. Put a little music
on. Or not. You are not alone.
You with your gash of diamonds
bound in a common fabric.
A man's infection lies inside you,
in petals of ash and abandoned
pages, the disinfected bucket
and scanned line, the sharp green scent
of lime on things that go unspoken.
In you, the decomposition
that winter brings to an end.
And in the sap that aches one
April over breakfast: you. You.
In the dinner passed in silence,
the distant shrieking of a swan.

Mallarmé

When I closed my eyes, a book opened
the way a chest opens for the surgeon
to lay the organ in, and because I could
not feel the flesh where once I lived or see
the words, the book began to read itself.
And then, it said, *an onyx vase appeared,
and the room, walled in mirrors, turned
to onyx, and the eye of the vase filled
with the ashes of rooms where once I lived.*
How anyone could see this and never see
their bodies in the glass, I cannot say,
how the gods of eyes float their angels.
But if they make the death of all who look
a summons, who remains to call it *pure*,
as oxygen is, breathed from a machine.
Who will close the book that cannot close
completely, cannot blind the vestibule,
jeweled in blood, longing to be stitched.

Poe

If you want to keep a soul alive,
seal it in a story, behind a wall,
and there will come a day you
cannot tell which wall from wall.
All are haunted now, which makes
your confession pointless, if
not incoherent, and the cop
folds up his notes, sighs, and leaves you
broken, scared, taking to heart
a frail romantic taste for pain.
No one to lay eyes or waste
or the wounded in their fevers.
Kids in leather and lotus-eaten
eyes remind you, the tattooed
figures of the talon and skull fit
into fiercely microscopic holes.
If you are high, the petals trail.
The firework of a moment ago
drops its slow and bony fingers.
The policeman leaves and leaves.
You sip your claret with a cat
who sleeps for the both of you,
because she is afraid of nothing,
as you too are afraid, nothing
before us, nothing after, but she
cannot, in her little head, hear
you scratch against the emptiness
the cold, white, benumbing cant
that is the grand tedium of seas,

the mesmerist whisper, the bell
that sizzles in the acid of its song.
She cannot fathom your addiction
where deep in every corpse is gold,
like hair in songs of inexperience,
each bitten sentiment anxious
to come clear as ghost, gas, totems
when you plague them, paramours
whose names foam the lips of oceans,
whose throats now are paper and swans
in the land where you go missing.

Zion

In a wasteland south of the Great Salt Lake,
the man on the cliff edge calls, his voice lost
in the echoes, each echo stranger than the last,
more removed from the throne and throat
of human error, so vast the emptiness I cannot
tell you what is echo, what a voice. Whose, the ear
that hangs a window on the view. One bird
becomes two, two—in silence—one, and still, to me,
the many. Where there is design, there is a story.
Where there is beauty, the ache of light that is
everywhere broken. Two birds become one,
one the many, a flock against the sheer indifferent
glory of the palisades. Where there is beauty,
there is the chaos of the beauty-shattered eye.
If you are coming, bring water, figs, strong shoes.
Bring a friend. I will bring the silence of one
friend who came and fell (or was it *jumped*) and just
kept falling, one day beneath the cliffs of Utah.

Stone

A child returns to her childhood
as blue does to a sky. Always more
to nightmare that is new. I cannot say,
still, which rock came from which child
in the storm of rocks, when I was small.
In war, you find parts impaled on sticks
at the entrance of the village. I have worn
that look, the missing part. I deserved it.
I tell myself. I cannot tell you why.
Some days, when I am walking, a rock falls
out of nowhere, and then, it disappears.
A sob of wind surges through the branches,
a face so blue it enters paradise unseen.

The Words

There will never be a Mediterranean
again without the thousand refugees
who drowned this week, never the same sun
to stamp the passport of the red horizon.
Never this night water, blacker than air.
Old sky falls to shoulder stars no longer
there, but here we are, on the open sea.
Here waves and invocations of a language
left to rummage heaven for our bearings.
Bodies break like starlight at the table,
and the old star says they are one body,
one sea where a thousand refugees go
nameless, and still they burn. Still the rain
sizzles and fades, and the beauty of our
knives comes and goes across the gutters.
What does it mean to pray for the dead.
Does the bended knee empower or calm
or frame vocations of the powerless.
Words like this fill with silent questions.
Names of thousands turn to smoke, ink,
everything that gives beneath the fathoms,
and I need them in times of speechlessness
and crisis. I need them to fail their calling
and call again. Whatever the cry for help
slipped into phones and bottles, whatever
I cast against the breakers to the other
shore, it washes back chiming, tolling.
Our skin breathes, it must, like the pages
that flutter one another as they fall.

The dead light up the skyline of our shelves,
but when a body reads, it reads alone.
Confusion closes its gash across the water.
A mast goes under. Histories end.
But the hopeful bound for shore remain
more distant than the dead will ever be.
Those I call departed, I call them *them*.
I make them out of memory and wish
like the refugee who bears a signature
of landfall refuge that never quite arrives.
I am counting the missing, one, one, one.
I am losing my place, beginning again.
And I know there will never be a sea
as vast as the disenfranchisement
of one. Never again a day like this.
And then, there is, engraved with names that drown
the face of grief, the moment it is named.

Vanitas

after Frances de la Tour

Take this night no larger than a room,
this Mary Magdalene drenched in shade,
no less than any skull or book, their image
dipped in the dimly burning waters
of a mirror, in the water-borne gaze
before the mirror that cannot look away.
Body, skull, and glass create a cradle
of hesitations, phantomed by a candle
partially eclipsed, the one they shelter,
revealed in the worship of obstacles
around it. What we do see is an arm,
a table, cheeks the pale tint of dawn,
the tip of the flame behind the skull
so close I fear the bone is catching fire.
Such is the collateral pleasure of nights
that call us in, to see her fingers read
the empty sockets, the way she rests them
there without horror or disavowal,
having come this far with a body that knows
what it is to burn, to suffer deeper
silences until death spoke in kindness.
All is vanity, it says, but why say it
over and over on permanent display
in the wings of this museum. Why
the guarded halls of the dead who lift
our eyes, bathed in fire without end.

III

Angel

I had a friend in school who found Christ
and lost touch with those who never did.
He was just that happy, he said, and walked
ablaze an inch or two from earth, and in
farewell he scratched a cruel note in my yearbook,
but we were kids, and maybe I deserved it,
and Christ was somewhere, in there, rummaging
hell and the human heart. I do not think
I envied him, but maybe. And *maybe* became
a general spirit like the air made breath
before we speak. Or the faces in a crowd
that become one face, one ghost, and boys
on stage stumble over words. Grace is a gift.
I learned that somewhere. And I believed it
just enough, as one believes, on some dark
street, alone, that soon the homes will dawn,
the smell of coffee will drift from room to room,
the Lord will roll us on our marble from dark
to light to the lighter falling of the shade.
I have been trying to pull my shadow from this
sack of blood and more acceptable behaviors,
but hell if it does not mouth these words
behind me. I say, forgive me for how I walk
all over you. And meanwhile a friend has
been talking my direction, when I was listening
to the general spirit. Let me be specific.
I wish I had been better to my grandmother.
If only I listened for the dead weight in her
anger and her stone opinions, the internment

of the breakdown in her strenuous laugh.
If silent grace gave children some asylum
from her voice, I do not blame the child.
If only I heard her silence inside mine.
I did. Years later, bearing gifts. Flowers.
When her face shattered into tears, we,
the children, were ushered far away.
In my silent church, the angels that bear
insipid smiles, they must be up to something,
up to their eyes in morphine and music
and the long dark history of their birth
in human flesh. Why else do they float
at death's approach. Or blow their trumpets
in the still air above the open casket.
The Jesus of my youth hung from his altar
like an elk, and angels framed the suffering
in precious stone. There is a better world,
and dying mothers look on it in fear.
And I to them. There is a better world,
and it is this that makes a hell of earth
where friends are scarce, saviors everywhere.
The children we become are ushered away,
and I see her still: the woman inside
the stiffer meaner one I knew. Christ,
I said. And if I prayed, it was a stranger
me talking to her, talking to no one in
particular. By which I mean, myself.
On the ride home, shadow of the poplars
swept the 60s. Silence felt personal,
and still more so as the shadows lengthened,
and as light withdrew, less and less.

Calvary

What you have heard is half-true, half-forgotten.
It's what we have, a rubric written in old
blood whose spirit of inclusion admits
the occasional invention, the apocryphal
goat at midnight, for one, who has broken
down the gate again, and wandered through
the refuse of our neighbors. Forgive him.
Him and the others of a now more distant
Jerusalem whose pattern of lesser hardships
and small routines goes largely unreported.
No less imagined than the clouds of certain
portraits of the killing, the same weather
that hung above the clueless who pulled in
their laundry, looking up to see future there.
What they do not know cannot save them.
Or bring them comfort. Or the vague weight
of clouds when they make a night of day.
Imagine then, once the body is deposed,
the men who take the burden on their shoulders
go nameless through the margins to the grave.
Take this young man, a soldier of low rank,
his wave of nausea slow to gather and withdraw
into the obscurities holy books are made of.
He is sitting beneath an olive tree, counting
coins, fouled with blood, less a true believer
in the entitlements of kings than an otherwise
impoverished soul with a wife, an oath, a child.
A drudge of circumstance. That is the story
he tells himself, and the need for the ever

better listener feels fundamental, as work is,
and wine at dusk, and whatever cut of meat
and means the heirs of grief and privilege refuse.

Air

1.

The holier the stone the more like stone
the power and resolve that laid it, there,
in the heart of the contested common.
The last of the temple King Solomon built.
So say the faithful in their signature black
though doubtless they understand: to build
a wall is no king's work, but that of servants
who will go nameless, and if another god
claims his prophet hitched here his horse
with wings, there is little to say to make
a god recant, revise, or otherwise move,
to abandon a place like that. The prayer
whispered or tucked into a hole in stone
might be, in installments, one long prayer,
incanted under the breath, and if it helps,
it helps, it mortars, mends, transmogrifies
the dullness of loss that makes a stone a stone,
a holy land a calf whose gold is blood.

2.

Every comic dies now and then, but then,
if called, they rise, and folks remember best
the deeply wounded ones who made them
laugh like friends. I am thinking of you,
Greg Giraldo, who told Joan Rivers once,
*You used to look your age, now you don't
even look your species.* And then her face—
wounded, tightened, paralyzed, stitched,
healed and babied with the finest lotions—
gave way, and I saw a little white light in
her teeth, a bit of joy, however nervously
touched, beyond the scalpel of this affront
or that desire to be young, I saw her death
in the arms of your addiction, the one
that took you too damn soon, to sit in heaven
and roast God, as your best friend put it,
as if nothing were sacred where everything is,
and each cold mask crumbles into laughter.

3.

When I think of idols that have died,
I think of the toy my father saved from
his childhood, how it reddened his shelf.
Beside his picture with the governor,
a small truck with no one in it. It served
as proof of the boy I never met, never
understood. He had so little child
in him, let alone the sentimental kind.
You should always keep one reminder,
he said. I always did, always thought
he loved me better when I was small.
Look at me, said all the rusted places.
And when he left us, they said it again,
look, but what they revealed remained
an empty promise. And I could see it,
touch it. It had wheels. Hollow places.
When I think of death, I think of this.
And it flew into walls and drove right through.

Fire Scripture

The death gods do not live here anymore.
        Codex after codex left the Mayan shores
for the cities of Europe by whose names
        we came to know one relic from another.
Missionaries burned the lion's share,
        and the natives watched. For months,
they grieved. The bell they raised went through
        the heavy motions, and no one came.
It tolled for them, and no one bothered
        looking up. They prayed. They died.
And what remained were artifacts, bells,
        the Madonna with her beloved dead
across her lap. And as she ran her fingers
        through his hair, so like a god of beauty
and horror all at once, she wept as one does
        at the power of singular hours.
And she said to him, let me tell you a story.
        Before you were born, I found a book
beside a stream beneath the olive trees.
        Discarded perhaps, I cannot know,
or left to console those who wander here
        to stare into the current to mend the mind
whose flesh is most water. The paper was bark,
        rough like the hands of a mason,
its call like a steeple's or a house in flames.
        And when I opened it, smoke poured out.
It frightened me, so I tried to close it.
        The scent of hair blackened my eyes,
and I smelled of it. I wept. You were less

  than a word back then, less than the blue
of paradise at the bottom of a well. Needless
  to say, I could not read. Or rather, I read,
in my blindness, what only smoke reveals.
  I read the way a body reads its world to live,
the way a river reads the lay of the land,
  or a shore the sea it strikes and voices.
Let me tell you. Before you were born,
  I laid before a book on fire. And breathed.

Sun

In Oregon once, the acolytes in saffron
sweatshirts and idolatrous medallions
made a vow to grow roots and change
address, to elect the man with the sunset
sport coat to serve as mayor and recast
community codes, to pull a nail here,
an ordinance there, the streets signs
of their Christian neighbors taken down
to make way for the Sanskrit of their master.
At last, the real estate of consciousness
was growing. Less in communal rapture
and rage that climaxed in bewildered tears
than the watchful stillness that came after.
Surely there was nobility in this.
The lotus of their suffering flush, effulgent.
Somewhere a ribcage cools in a field,
stoned on love, that kind that lifts the fog
above its place on earth, but after that,
what? *The new human*, the archetype
their teacher promised, what they were hoping
to become, what they feared the locals
in hunting gear and office would destroy?
And can you blame them. Say a torch
broke the glass of your hotel in Portland
or a long sleeve poisoned the salad bars
of your town cafés. Who would not feel
some shadow of their partisan nature fall
into the arms of your frightened kind.
I have been that child, that prideful victim

of my own outrage. Call it the fitful
cleansing of a birthmark, the forever
failed extradition of histories of abuse.
Call it shell-shock; or war; or call it
what it is, salmonella and kerosene
and the scarlet seam of the unclean
lesion breaking, but do not call it new.
Puritans of permission raise their cries
as Christ does at the altar, disseminating
wine with a bitter summons to forgive.
Submission and refusal. How better
to survive the next ice age or spiritual
contagion: a thicker coat, warmer meal,
a feast day between tribes; how better to live
and let live than deep inside a system
of guards to wave friends and family through.
The body of the chosen is a body
after all, and so in need of water, harbor,
seasonal fire and the couriers of sleep.
It shrouds itself in skin, as Bibles do,
and great redwoods, and the *new human*
laid beneath their limbs, a child of heaven
awakened from a scare to find herself,
transfixed, in a crystal of estrangement,
christened in the amber of dusk and dawn.

Behemoth

> *alles ist weniger, als*
> *es ist,*
> *alles ist mehr.*
> —Paul Celan

1.

Then the Lord replied, *who are you*
to question me. Look at what I made.
Consider the behemoth, its sinew, thigh,
the great gray tail that sways like a cedar.
Take these hills that lay their oranges
and grasses at your feet. And Job fell
silent. The startled flowers of the field
shot their arrows in his eyes. Sun ached,
faded, ached, swelled and all that passed
unsaid rose and fell through the willows.
Then Job looked into the scars of boils
written in his hands and gripped them closed.
Moths stormed the river with their gold
dust, and the water startled briefly, gold.

2.

I like my testament battered, abused,
scored with a dozen questions in the margins.
Make that five million. *Why bother
with damnation*, I ask the behemoth,
and the words float out as the scented
paths of smoke in some cathedrals do,
or someone silent on the phone in shock,
waiting for news that never quite arrives.
One soul turns to the greater figure,
confused—it happens over and over—
one plus one plus one and so on,
and you know you will never get there.
One plus one plus one, the Lord whispers
to the world of us. Or one such world.

3.

A writer writes, *Nah sind wir, Herr*,
and reads it back aloud, alone, eyes
closed, the exhalation of the word
Herr a leaden burden he lays down
in a small dark inner court of appeals.
The exhibition table sags with words.
If it please the court, the writer writes,
and the stenographer reads them back.
Lord, we have kneeled over the ditch,
and the blood cast your image into us.
If it please the court, the writer writes,
it is our *blood. Pray to* us. And no one
answers. *Us*, he says, a little softer,
sweeter, darker. And the clock goes still.

4.

After a great suffering, sometimes a god,
sometimes a god-like emptiness. Night
scatters diamonds and says, the hell with it,
take them, take them all. I know a woman
who lost her faith and spoke of it in cold
tones I learned to love. It made her gaze
abstract and gave five million missing
a face. I want to say God loves the godless,
but what do I know. You talk to the dead,
and the dark unknowing opens its arms
and says, you there, believer, you too,
nonetheless. And something burns away
between you and a woman. Perhaps a god-
like fog. But that is least of your concerns.

5.

Always another monster in the room.
I tell myself that much—when I am angry
and afraid—and there are always two.
There are no facts anymore, says the man
who cuts my hair, and the gray snow falls.
The Jews control everything these days.
Then silence hangs in the air a moment.
I want to say it makes a statement. Truth is,
it flows, untouched, into a second silence
where there are always two. Fire taught me,
long ago there was a column of smoke.
Enough now to fill a library with dark.
And as it disappeared, it smelled like hair.
Like hair, it withered, stretching out for miles.

6.

When photos of a million horrors
made the papers, a million eyes stopped
and stared, the way a glass of water stares,
and the railcar around it coming to rest.
The poet laid down her pen, took it in
her hand, laid it down again. Readers
looked up from philosophies that end
where knowledge ends and keeps on ending.
Words *broke down*, aka *wept, confessed,
lost their shit, their rational composure*.
They remembered just so much and sang
we will not forget, and when words failed,
music shadowed them a while, and failed,
as echoes do in halls of state and worship.

7.

A man opens his mouth, and out it comes,
ash, wind, pleasantry, ash. *Pray to us*,
he says alone, aloud, and the lightness
blows to tatters. If the threnody feels
too lovely, well, tough. If a song buries
its message in the music. Are we so small
in the clouds of smoke, they swallow us.
Are we that ashamed, embittered, proud.
Does the angel's sword chill our necks.
Is it any wonder a survivor grows more
critical, easily wounded, his testament
bent brightly in the vise. If the music is
unlovely, tough. If later on, it flowers,
if the ash makes visible the air we breathe.

8.

After the behemoth lay down and stars
followed and the general with his lover
drank their potion in the bunker, a new
animal appeared. Or rather a revenant
of the familiar. Same tusk, same haunch,
same bold shoulder, and although a ghost,
you could feel it settle over the horizon.
Or turn the head to its pillow or a deer
to the scent of fire. When, one night,
it roared, we felt the cry lie down in our
children. Though we never spoke of it.
And when they sang in school, we did not weep.
Or if we did, we kept it to ourselves.
We opened our mouths. To let the music in.